NYC SCENES
Coloring Pages

Sketches In and Around Manhattan

by
Whitney Grimes

Copyright © 2016 Whitney Grimes, All rights reserved.

You may photocopy the images in this book for your own personal use and to color-in. You may display pictures that you have colored-in on social media or your own website with the condition that you attribute the original art to Whitney Grimes.

Aside from the exceptions above, no part of this publication may be reproduced, published, or displayed without advance written permission from Whitney Grimes. These images and designs may not be resold or used in any commercial endeavor unless specifically approved, in writing and in advance, by Whitney Grimes.

You can contact Whitney at hellowhitneygrimes@gmail.com

ISBN-13: 978-1530452682
ISBN-10: 1530452686

Be sure to visit

WhitneyGrimes.com

This book belongs to

_____

Table of Contents

1. Sixth Avenue facing Jefferson Market Library Clocktower, West Village
2. Meatball Pizza (Posto) on Second Avenue, Gramercy
3. Flower Studio on Greenwich Avenue, Greenwich Village
4. Brooklyn Bridge and Manhattan Bridge from atop Cliff Street, FiDi (Financial District)
5. Sneakers on a traffic light, SoHo
6. Skyline from the Hudson River aboard the Honorable William Wall
7. Lower Bar Entrance, Lower East Side
8. Madison Square Park Fountain (for lucky wishes)
9. View of West Village from my roof, East Village
10. Grafitti on Restaurant (Cacio e Pepe), East Village
11. Chinatown
12. 9th Street Path Station entrance, West Village
13. Rainy Day with Cecile on Fifth Avenue, West Village
14. Washington Square Park Fountain
15. Boat Pond, Central Park
16. Skateboard Session, Union Square Park
17. Flatiron
18. Bike Path, Battery Park City
19. Jimmy Pump Party, Gramercy
20. Let's Go Rangers!, Bryant Park
21. New York Public Library Lion, Bryant Park
22. The Statue of Liberty
23. Rockefeller Center Ice Rink, Midtown
24. Red Hook, Brooklyn
25. Empire State Building, Midtown
26. Fire Station, Downtown
27. Freedom Tower and Brookfield Place, FiDi (Financial District)
28. DUMBO (Down Under the Brooklyn Bridge), Brooklyn
29. Caren and Melissa on the roof, East Village
30. Sunny's Bar in Red Hook, Brooklyn
31. Staten Island Ferry
32. Times Square, Midtown
33. Yankees Stadium entrance Gate 4, The Bronx
34. The Lowline Lab on Essex Street, Lower East Side
35. Map of NYC

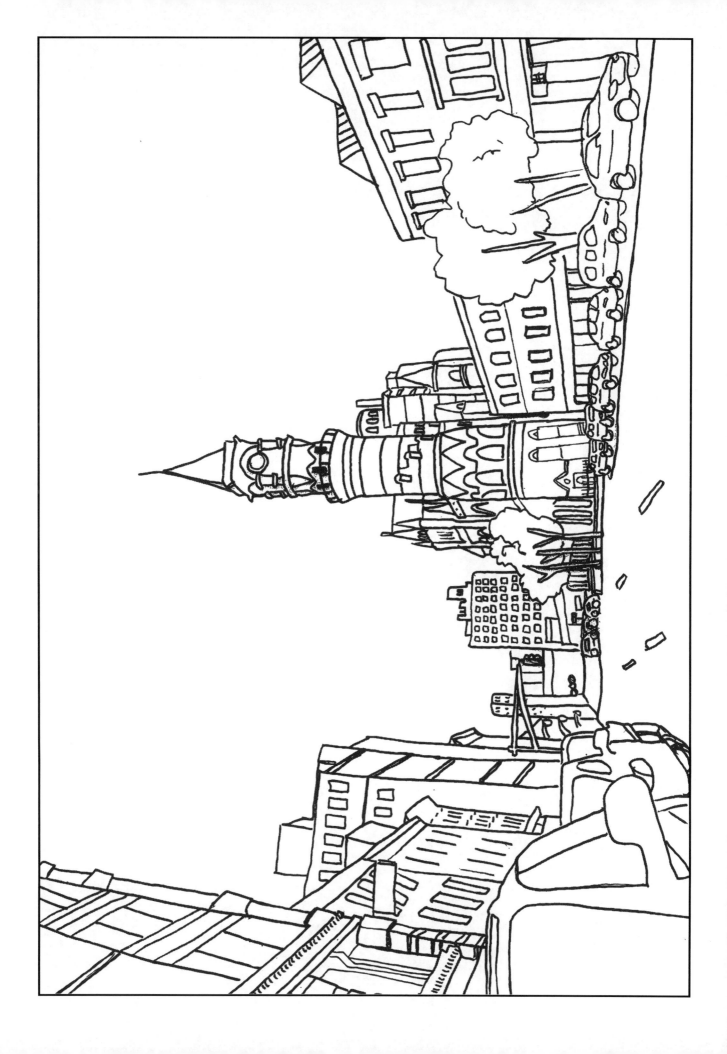

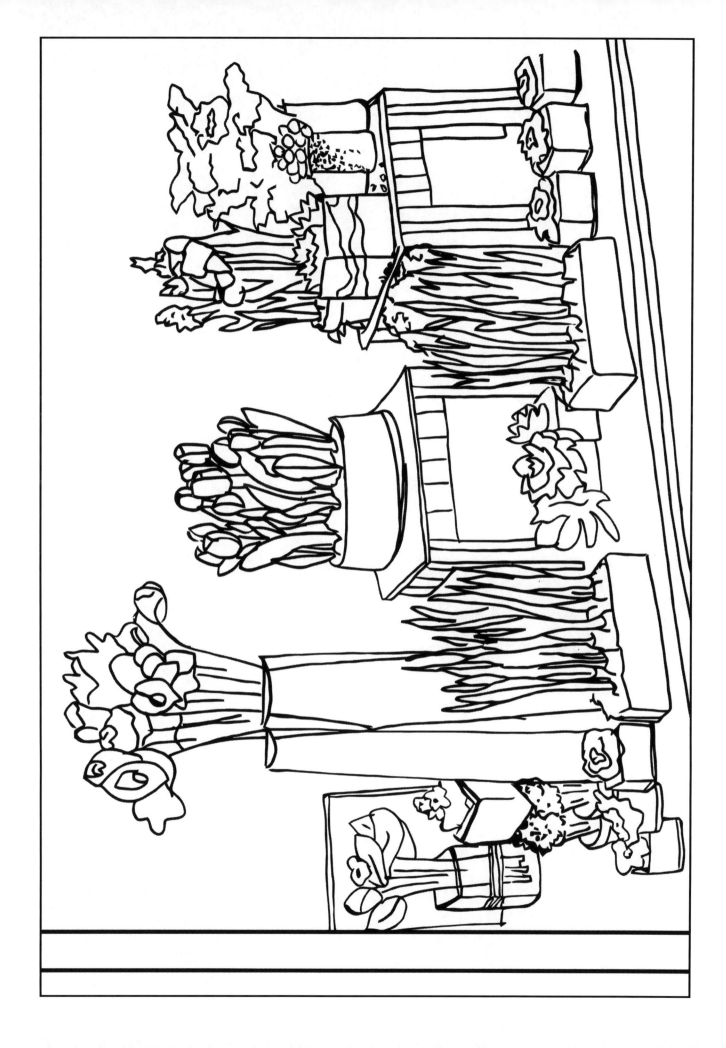

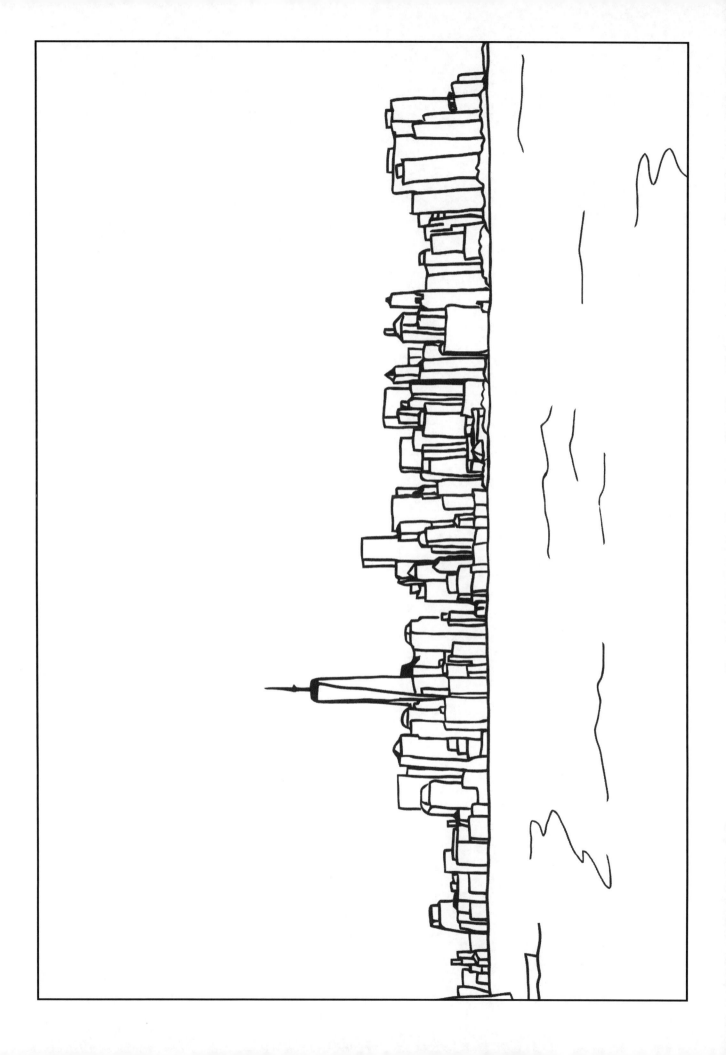

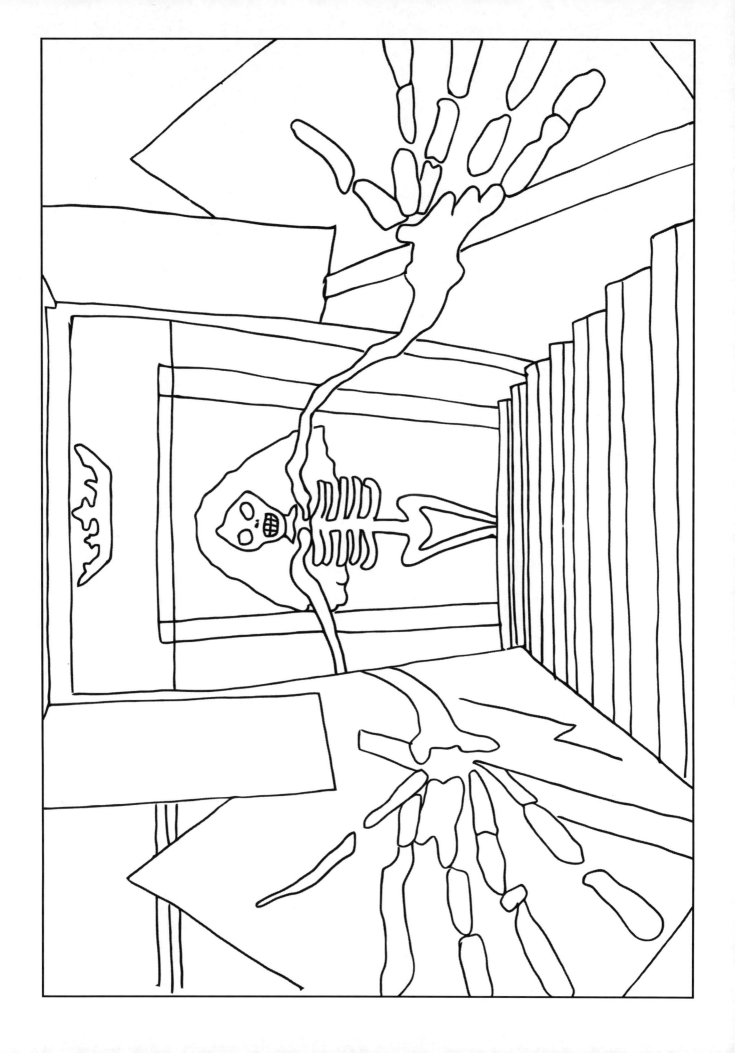

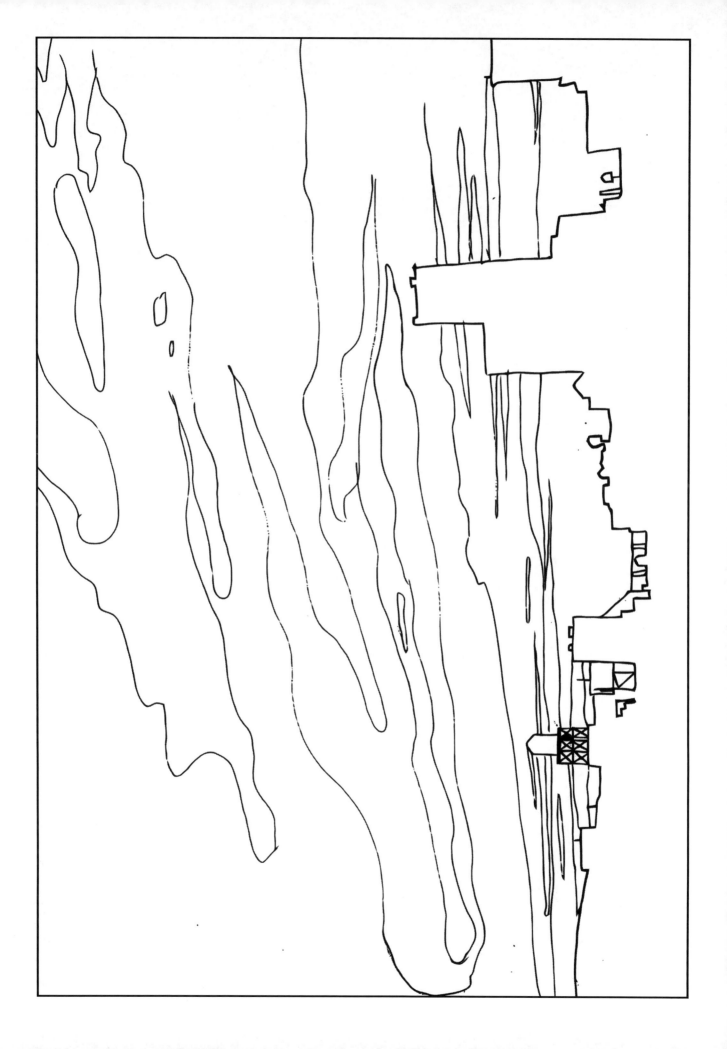

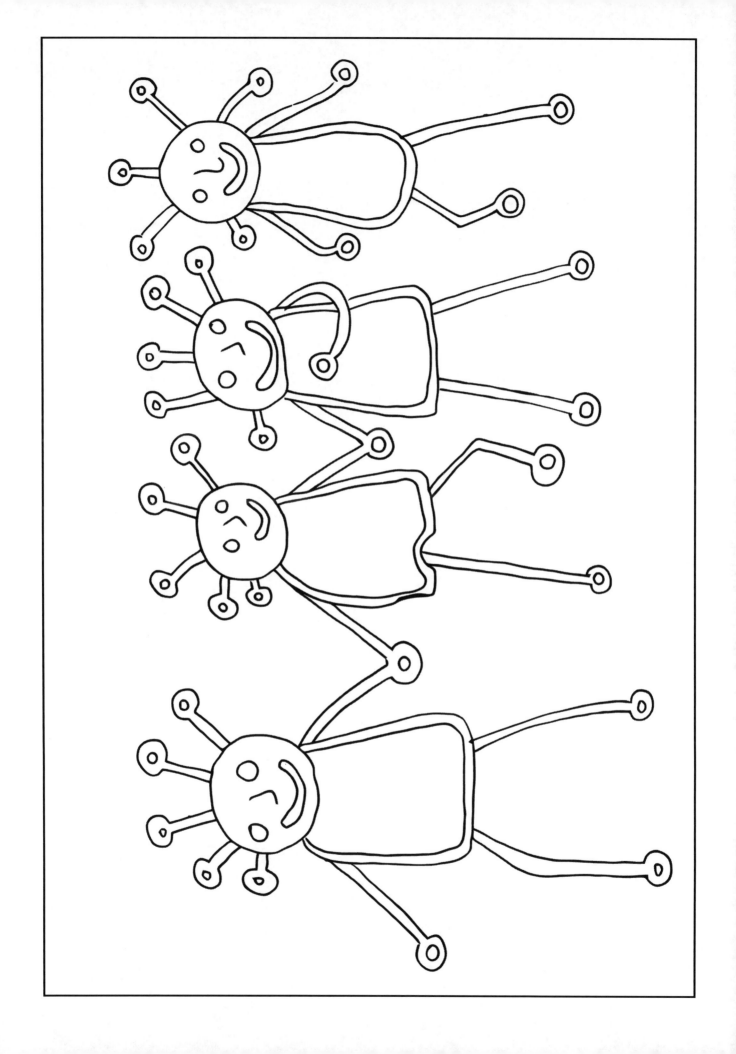

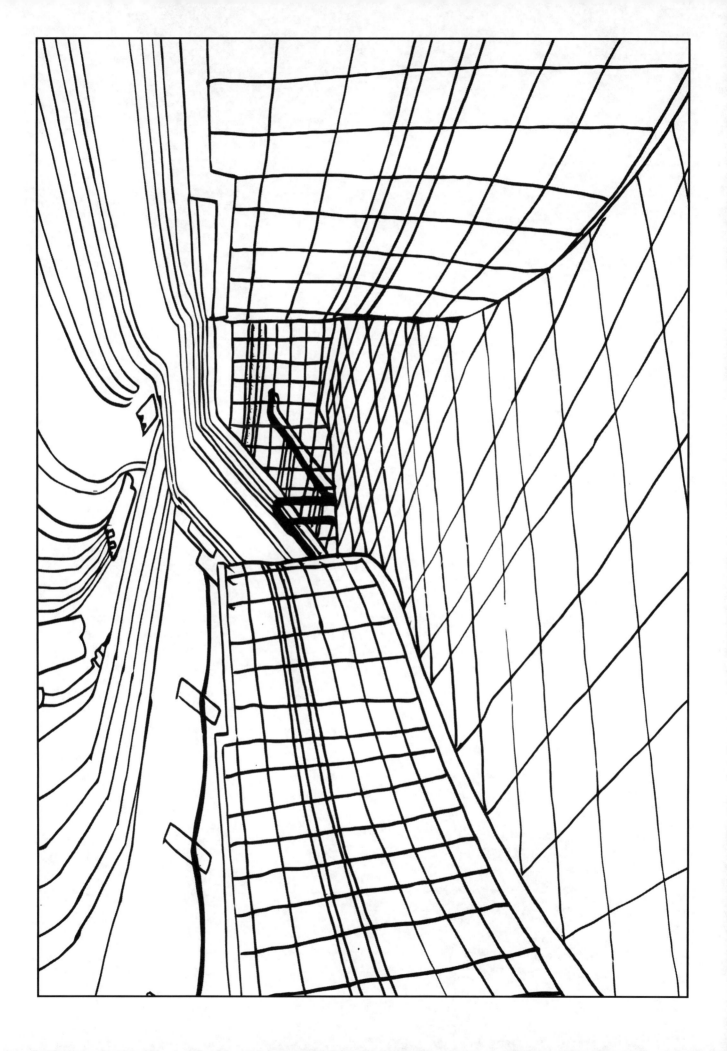

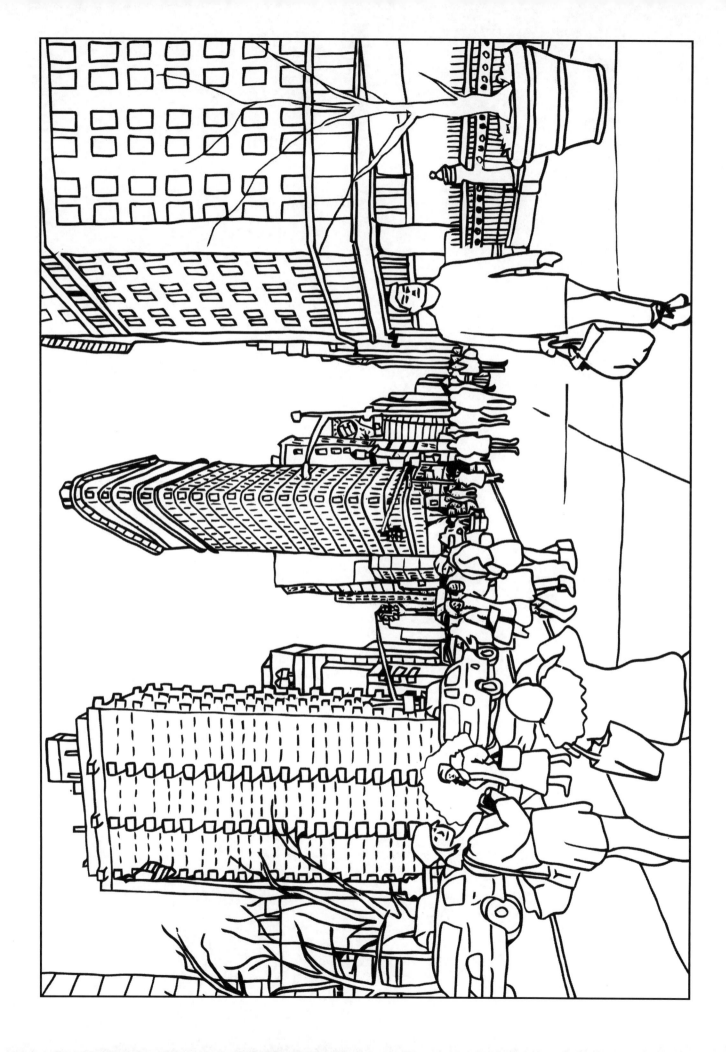

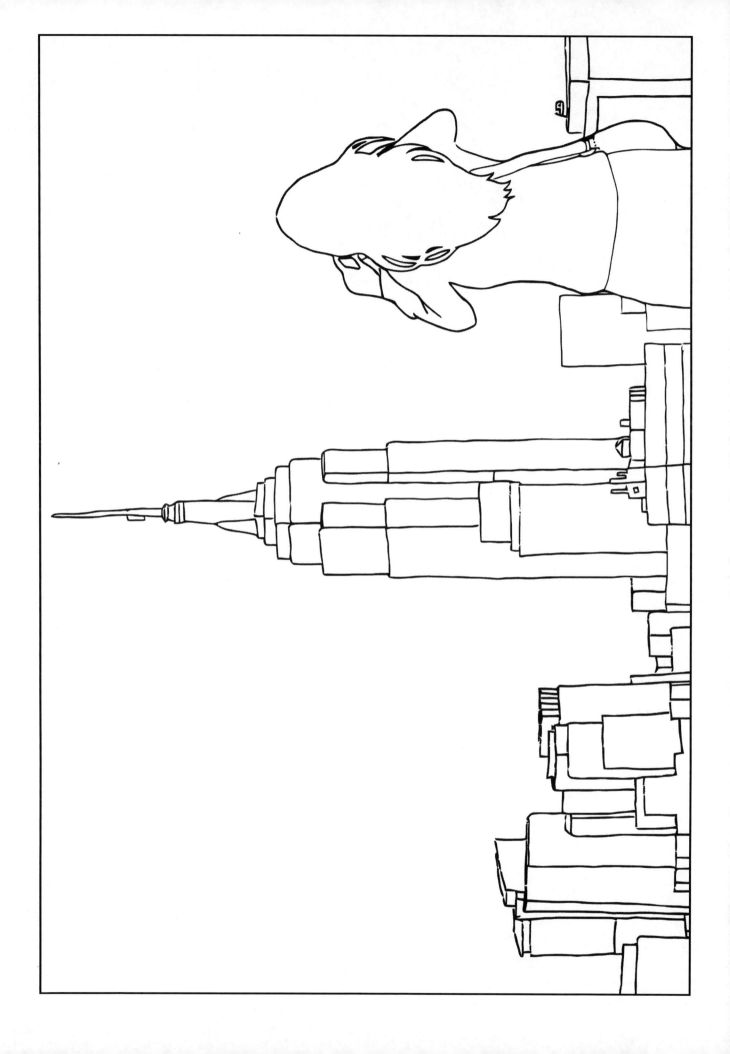

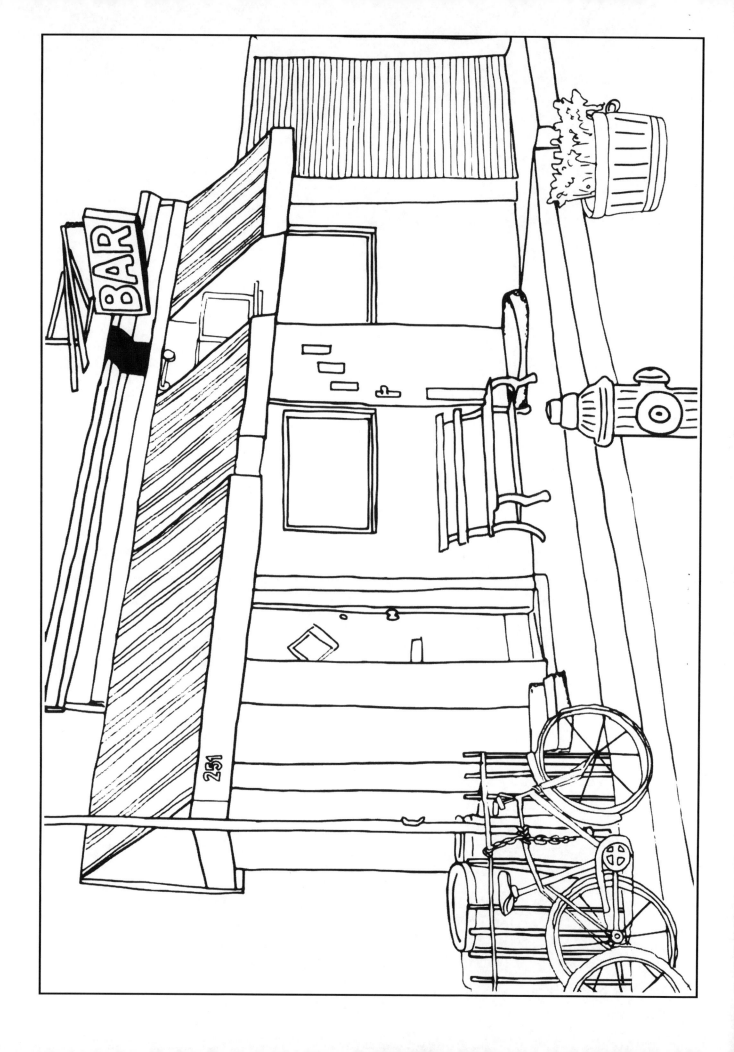

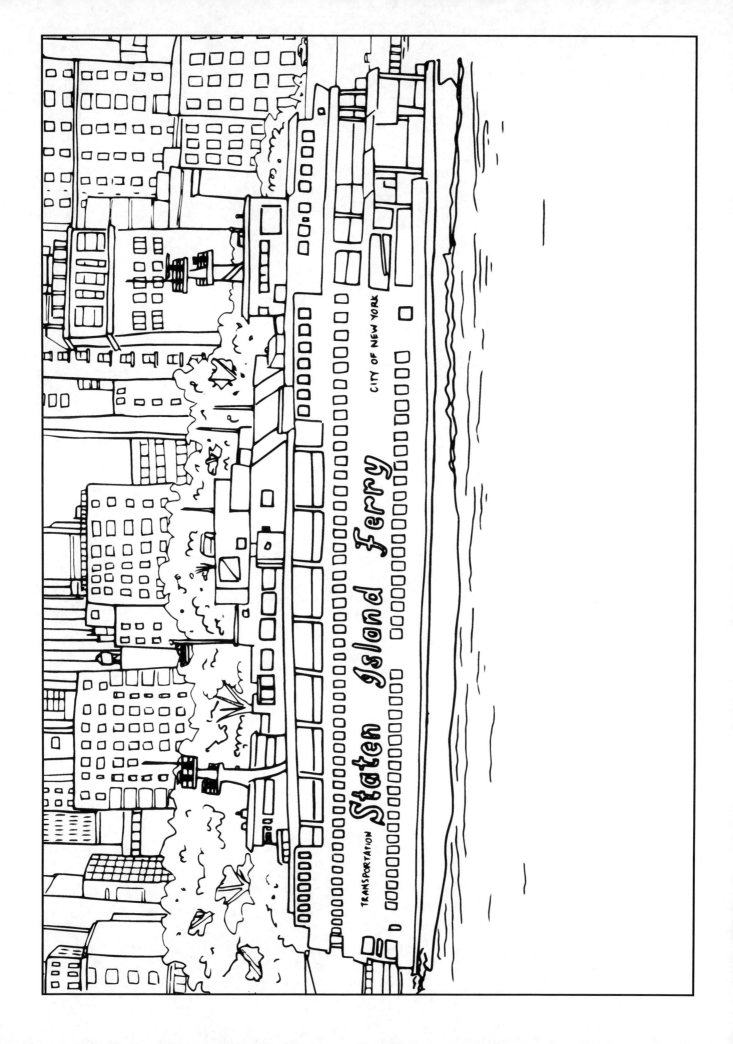
TRANSPORTATION
Staten Island Ferry
CITY OF NEW YORK

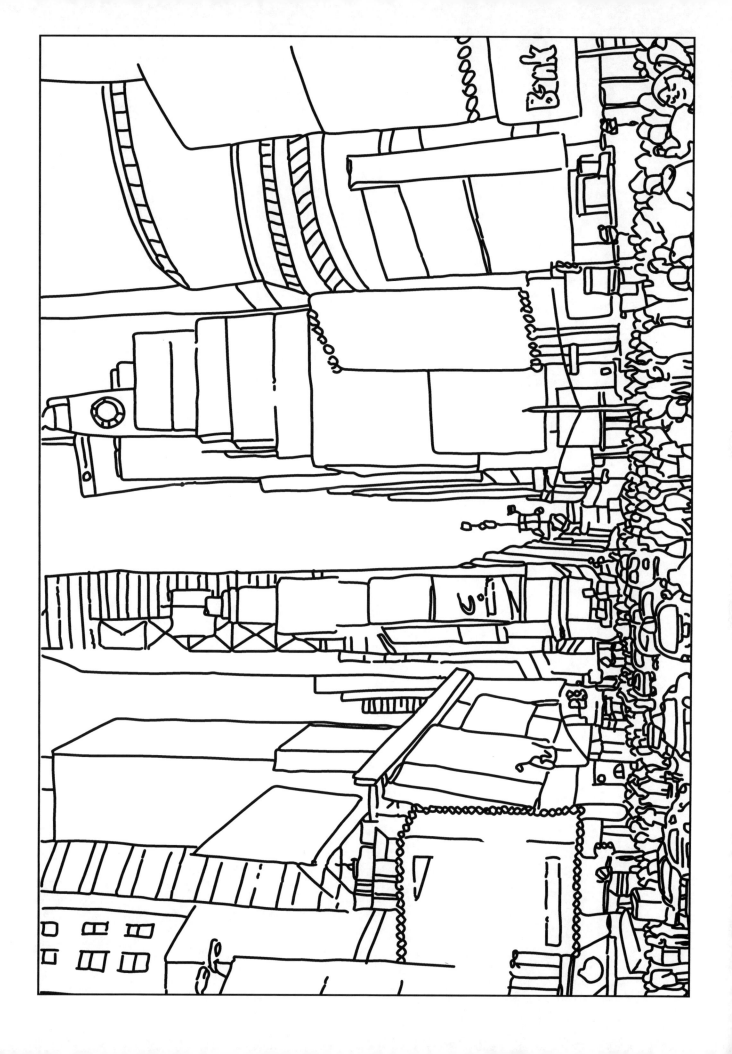

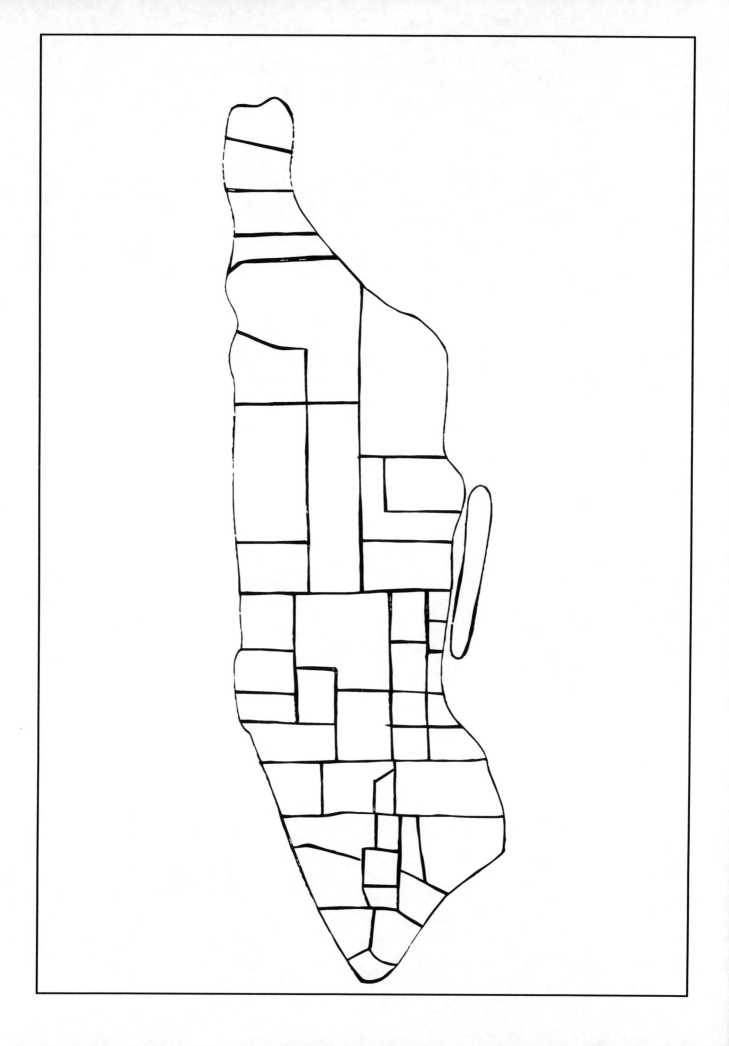

In her free time, Whitney Grimes can be found taking adventures around her neighborhood. Occasionally venturing around Manhattan and surrounding boroughs. Whitney loves to explore new places around the world, looking for beauty in ordinarily overlooked places.

Follow me on
Instagram: hellowhitneygrimes
Facebook: https://www.facebook.com/whitney.grimes.58

Made in the USA
Lexington, KY
15 April 2016